# PASSIVE INCOME PULSE

### Real Estate Tactics for Thriving in Today's Market

**NELLA BYRAN**

## Copyright

**No part of this should be reproduced without the permission of the author.**

© Nella Byran 2024

# Contents

Introduction..................................................................4

Understanding the Passive Income Paradigm.....................8

Navigating Today's Real Estate Landscape.......................11

Building Your Investment Foundation ..............................14

Leveraging Rental Properties for Passive Income.............19

Exploring Fix-and-Flip Strategies .....................................24

Harnessing the Power of Short-Term Rentals ...................28

Maximizing Returns with Commercial Properties ............33

Uncovering Opportunities in Emerging Markets ..............37

The Art of Negotiation in Real Estate Deals .....................41

Mitigating Risks and Protecting Your Investments...........47

Scaling Your Portfolio for Long-Term Success ................54

Embracing Technology for Property Management ...........60

Creating Passive Income Streams with Real Estate Syndication ......................................................................65

Tax Strategies for Real Estate Investors...........................70

The Future of Passive Income in Real Estate ...................75

Conclusion......................................................................80

# Introduction

In the pulsating world of real estate investment, where every transaction reverberates with potential, lies the promise of a lifestyle defined by financial freedom, security, and prosperity. Welcome to "Passive Income Pulse: Real Estate Tactics for Thriving in Today's Market," your definitive guide to navigating the dynamic landscape of real estate investment to secure a future brimming with passive income streams.

This book is your compass in the labyrinth of modern real estate, where traditional norms intersect with cutting-edge strategies, and where the savvy investor can carve out their path to success. Within these pages, you'll discover a comprehensive roadmap designed to equip you with the knowledge, tools, and mindset necessary to thrive in today's ever-evolving market.

Our journey begins with a fundamental shift in perspective - understanding the Passive Income Paradigm. Here, we'll redefine your approach to wealth creation, illuminating the transformative power of generating income while you sleep. From there, we'll embark on a guided tour through the intricacies of today's real estate landscape, navigating the twists and turns with confidence and insight.

With a solid foundation in place, we'll delve into the core principles of building your investment foundation. From leveraging rental properties to exploring fix-and-flip strategies, each chapter is a building block in your path to financial independence. We'll harness the power of short-term rentals, maximize returns with commercial properties, and uncover opportunities in emerging markets, all while honing the art of negotiation to secure the best deals.

But success in real estate is not without its risks. That's why we'll devote ample attention to mitigating risks and protecting your investments, ensuring that your hard-earned wealth is safeguarded against the unpredictable currents of the market. And as you scale your portfolio for long-term success, we'll explore the role of technology in property management, harnessing its potential to streamline operations and amplify your returns.

No discussion of real estate investment would be complete without addressing the critical issue of taxation. That's why we'll dive into tax strategies specifically tailored for real estate investors, providing you with the knowledge to optimize your returns and minimize your liabilities.

Finally, we'll peer into the future of passive income in real estate, exploring emerging trends, technologies, and opportunities on the horizon. Armed with this foresight, you'll be poised to capitalize on tomorrow's trends today, ensuring your continued success in an ever-evolving market.

So, whether you're a seasoned investor looking to expand your portfolio or a newcomer eager to embark on your journey to financial independence, "Passive Income Pulse" is your indispensable companion. Let's embark on this journey together, as we unlock the secrets to thriving in today's dynamic real estate market.

# Understanding the Passive Income Paradigm

In the realm of wealth creation, the concept of passive income stands as a beacon of financial freedom, offering individuals the opportunity to break free from the constraints of traditional employment and embrace a life of abundance and autonomy. But what exactly is passive income, and how does it differ from the conventional model of earning a living?

Passive income, at its core, is income that is earned with minimal effort or active involvement on the part of the recipient. Unlike the linear model of earning a paycheck in exchange for hours worked, passive income flows continuously, whether you're actively working or not. It is the ultimate manifestation of the adage "make money while you sleep," representing a paradigm shift in how we perceive and pursue financial success.

Passive income can be derived from a variety of sources, each with its own unique characteristics and potential for wealth generation. From rental properties and dividend-paying stocks to royalties from intellectual property and income generated from online businesses, the possibilities are limited only by your imagination and ingenuity.

The allure of passive income lies not only in its potential for financial gain but also in the freedom and flexibility it affords. By diversifying your income streams and reducing reliance on active labor, you can reclaim your time and energy to pursue your passions, spend time with loved ones, and cultivate a life of fulfillment and purpose.

Creating a sustainable passive income portfolio requires careful planning, diligence, and foresight. Building your portfolio from the ground up involves identifying lucrative investment opportunities, leveraging the power of compounding returns, and optimizing your asset allocation to maximize long-term growth.

Despite its undeniable appeal, passive income is often misunderstood and misconstrued. Common myths and misconceptions surrounding passive income can hinder progress towards financial freedom. By debunking these myths and gaining clarity on the realities of passive income, individuals can approach wealth creation with confidence and determination.

"Understanding the Passive Income Paradigm" is not just a chapter in a book; it's a mindset shift, a call to action, and a roadmap to financial freedom. By embracing the principles and practices outlined within these pages, individuals can unlock the door to a future defined by abundance, autonomy, and limitless opportunity. So, join us as we embark on this journey together, and let's chart a course towards a brighter, more prosperous tomorrow.

# Navigating Today's Real Estate Landscape

In the ever-evolving realm of real estate investment, navigating today's landscape requires a blend of adaptability, foresight, and strategic acumen. The dynamics of the market are in constant flux, shaped by economic trends, technological advancements, and shifting consumer preferences. To succeed in this multifaceted terrain, investors must possess a keen understanding of the forces at play and the agility to pivot in response to changing conditions.

Today's real estate landscape is characterized by both opportunities and challenges. On one hand, rapid urbanization, population growth, and evolving demographics continue to fuel demand for housing and commercial spaces. On the other hand, fluctuating interest rates, regulatory changes, and geopolitical uncertainties introduce elements of volatility and risk.

Amidst this backdrop, successful investors employ a multifaceted approach to navigating the complexities of the real estate market. They conduct thorough market research and analysis to identify emerging trends and untapped opportunities. They leverage technology and data analytics to gain insights into market dynamics and make informed decisions. They cultivate strategic partnerships and networks to access deal flow and unlock synergies. And they remain vigilant and adaptable, ready to adjust their strategies in response to evolving market conditions.

Central to navigating today's real estate landscape is the ability to identify and capitalize on market inefficiencies and dislocations. Whether it's uncovering undervalued properties in emerging neighborhoods, identifying distressed assets ripe for rehabilitation, or tapping into niche markets with high growth potential, successful investors possess the vision and insight to spot opportunities where others may see challenges.

Moreover, navigating today's real estate landscape requires a holistic approach that takes into account not only financial considerations but also environmental, social, and governance (ESG) factors. Sustainability, resilience, and social impact are increasingly important considerations for investors seeking to create long-term value and mitigate risk in their real estate portfolios.

In summary, navigating today's real estate landscape is a dynamic and multifaceted endeavor that requires a blend of strategic vision, market savvy, and adaptability. By staying informed, leveraging technology, cultivating strategic partnerships, and embracing a holistic approach to investment, investors can position themselves to thrive in the ever-changing world of real estate.

# Building Your Investment Foundation

Building a solid investment foundation in real estate is essential for long-term success and financial stability. It requires careful planning, diligent research, and strategic decision-making. Here's a comprehensive guide on how to build your investment foundation in real estate:

**Define Your Investment Goals**

Before diving into real estate investment, it's crucial to define your investment goals. Are you looking for steady rental income, long-term appreciation, or a combination of both? Clarifying your objectives will help guide your investment strategy and shape your decisions moving forward.

**Assess Your Risk Tolerance**

Real estate investment comes with inherent risks, including market fluctuations, tenant turnover, and unexpected expenses. Assess your risk tolerance and determine how much risk you're willing to take on. This will inform your investment strategy and asset allocation decisions.

**Educate Yourself**

Knowledge is power in real estate investment. Take the time to educate yourself about the fundamentals of real estate, including market dynamics, property valuation, financing options, and legal considerations. Attend seminars, read books, and seek advice from experienced investors to broaden your understanding.

**Establish Your Budget**

Determine how much capital you have available to invest in real estate. Consider your savings, investment accounts, and potential financing options such as mortgages or loans. Establishing a clear budget will help you narrow down your investment options and make informed decisions.

**Conduct Market Research**

Research is key to identifying lucrative investment opportunities. Analyze local real estate markets to identify areas with strong demand, favorable rental yields, and potential for appreciation. Consider factors such as population growth, job market trends, infrastructure development, and amenities.

**Identify Investment Strategies**

There are various investment strategies in real estate, including rental properties, fix-and-flip projects, commercial properties, vacation rentals, and real estate investment trusts (REITs). Evaluate each strategy based on your investment goals, risk tolerance, and market conditions to determine which aligns best with your objectives.

**Network with Professionals**

Building relationships with real estate professionals can provide valuable insights and opportunities. Connect with real estate agents, brokers, property managers, contractors, lenders, and other industry professionals to expand your network and access resources and expertise.

**Conduct Due Diligence**

Before making any investment decisions, conduct thorough due diligence on potential properties or projects. Evaluate factors such as property condition, location, rental income potential, expenses, market comparables, and legal considerations. Engage professionals such as inspectors, appraisers, and attorneys to assist with due diligence efforts.

**Secure Financing**

If you require financing for your real estate investment, explore financing options such as mortgages, loans, or partnerships. Compare interest rates, terms, and fees from multiple lenders to secure the most favorable financing arrangement for your investment.

**Create a Diversified Portfolio**

Diversification is key to mitigating risk and maximizing returns in real estate investment. Consider diversifying your portfolio across different property types, locations, and investment strategies to spread risk and capture opportunities in various market conditions.

By following these steps and building a strong investment foundation, you'll be well-positioned to embark on your real estate investment journey with confidence and clarity. Remember to stay disciplined, patient, and adaptable as you navigate the complexities of the real estate market.

# Leveraging Rental Properties for Passive Income

Leveraging rental properties for passive income is a tried-and-true strategy that offers investors the opportunity to generate steady cash flow while building long-term wealth. Here's a detailed guide on how to effectively leverage rental properties for passive income:

**Market Research and Property Selection**

Conduct thorough market research to identify areas with strong rental demand, favorable vacancy rates, and potential for rental income growth. Analyze factors such as population trends, employment opportunities, amenities, and school districts. Once you've identified target markets, carefully select rental properties that align with your investment goals, budget, and risk tolerance.

## Financial Analysis

Perform detailed financial analysis to assess the investment potential of rental properties. Calculate key metrics such as cash-on-cash return, cap rate, and gross rent multiplier to evaluate the profitability of potential investments. Consider factors such as purchase price, rental income, operating expenses, property taxes, insurance, and maintenance costs.

## Property Acquisition and Financing

Once you've identified a suitable rental property, explore financing options such as mortgages, loans, or partnerships to acquire the property. Compare interest rates, loan terms, and down payment requirements from multiple lenders to secure the most favorable financing arrangement. Conduct due diligence on the property to ensure it meets your investment criteria and aligns with your long-term objectives.

## Property Management

Effective property management is essential for maximizing rental income and ensuring tenant satisfaction. Consider whether you'll manage the property yourself or hire a professional property management company to handle day-to-day operations such as tenant screening, rent collection, maintenance, repairs, and lease enforcement. Establish clear communication channels with tenants and address any issues promptly to maintain positive landlord-tenant relationships.

## Tenant Screening and Lease Agreements

Screen prospective tenants thoroughly to minimize the risk of rental defaults, property damage, or eviction proceedings. Conduct background checks, verify employment and income, and obtain references from previous landlords to assess tenant suitability. Draft comprehensive lease agreements that outline rental terms, payment schedules, responsibilities, and expectations for both landlords and tenants. Ensure compliance with local landlord-tenant laws and regulations to protect your interests and mitigate legal risks.

**Rental Income Optimization**

Continuously monitor rental market conditions and adjust rental rates accordingly to optimize rental income. Enhance property appeal by making strategic upgrades or renovations to attract high-quality tenants and command higher rents. Implement cost-effective strategies to minimize vacancy periods and maximize occupancy rates, such as offering incentives to prospective tenants or marketing the property through various channels.

**Financial Management and Record-Keeping**

Maintain accurate financial records and track income and expenses related to the rental property. Establish a separate bank account for rental income and expenses to streamline financial management and facilitate tax reporting. Monitor cash flow regularly and set aside reserves for unforeseen expenses or vacancies. Consider consulting with a financial advisor or accountant to optimize tax efficiency and maximize deductions related to rental property ownership.

**Long-Term Planning and Portfolio Growth**

Develop a long-term investment strategy that aligns with your financial goals and risk tolerance. Consider diversifying your rental property portfolio across different property types, locations, and markets to spread risk and capture opportunities for growth. Reinvest rental income and profits into additional properties or asset classes to expand your portfolio and accelerate wealth accumulation over time.

By following these steps and implementing sound management practices, you can leverage rental properties to generate passive income and build a resilient investment portfolio that stands the test of time.

## Exploring Fix-and-Flip Strategies

Exploring fix-and-flip strategies in real estate investment involves identifying distressed properties, renovating them to increase their value, and then selling them for a profit. This strategy can be lucrative but requires careful planning, execution, and market knowledge.

Firstly, identify potential properties that are distressed, such as foreclosures, bank-owned properties, or homes in need of significant repairs. These properties are typically sold at a discount but have the potential for value appreciation through renovation.

Once you've identified a potential property, conduct a thorough inspection and assessment to determine the scope of renovations needed and estimate the cost of repairs. Consider factors such as structural integrity, mechanical systems, and cosmetic improvements to develop a comprehensive renovation plan.

Next, create a detailed budget and timeline for the renovation project, taking into account materials, labor costs, permits, and other expenses. It's essential to ensure that your budget allows for a sufficient margin of profit while still accounting for unexpected costs that may arise during the renovation process.

Assemble a team of qualified contractors, architects, and designers to execute the renovation project efficiently and to a high standard of quality. Establish clear communication channels and timelines to keep the project on track and within budget.

During the renovation process, focus on making strategic improvements that will add value to the property and appeal to potential buyers. This may include upgrading kitchens and bathrooms, improving curb appeal, updating flooring and fixtures, and addressing any structural or safety concerns.

Once the renovation is complete, market the property effectively to attract potential buyers and maximize your selling price. Utilize professional photography, staging, and online marketing channels to showcase the property's features and highlight its potential.

When negotiating offers from prospective buyers, be prepared to negotiate and consider factors such as market conditions, comparable sales, and the property's unique features. Ultimately, aim to sell the property for a price that provides a satisfactory return on your investment while still appealing to buyers.

Finally, ensure a smooth closing process by working closely with real estate professionals, attorneys, and title companies to finalize the sale and transfer ownership of the property. Celebrate your success and reinvest your profits into additional fix-and-flip projects or other investment opportunities to continue growing your real estate portfolio.

In summary, exploring fix-and-flip strategies in real estate investment requires careful planning, execution, and market savvy. By identifying distressed properties, renovating them strategically, and selling them for a profit, investors can capitalize on opportunities to generate significant returns and build wealth over time.

# Harnessing the Power of Short-Term Rentals

Harnessing the power of short-term rentals in real estate investment involves renting out properties for shorter durations, typically on a nightly or weekly basis, to travelers and vacationers. This strategy has gained popularity in recent years due to the rise of online platforms like Airbnb, which provide a convenient way for property owners to market their rentals and connect with potential guests. Here's a detailed look at how to effectively leverage short-term rentals:

**Property Selection**

Choose properties that are well-suited for short-term rentals, such as vacation homes, condos, apartments, or single-family residences in desirable locations. Consider factors such as proximity to tourist attractions, amenities, accessibility, and local regulations governing short-term rentals.

## Market Research

Conduct market research to identify demand for short-term rentals in your target location. Analyze factors such as tourism trends, seasonal fluctuations, occupancy rates, and average rental rates to assess the potential profitability of short-term rental properties.

## Property Preparation

Prepare your property for short-term rentals by furnishing it with comfortable and functional furniture, amenities, and essentials for guests. Create a welcoming and inviting atmosphere that enhances the guest experience and encourages positive reviews and repeat bookings.

## Listing Optimization

Create compelling and visually appealing listings for your short-term rental properties on online platforms like Airbnb, VRBO, or Booking.com. Use high-quality photos, detailed descriptions, and accurate pricing to showcase your property's unique features and attract potential guests.

**Guest Communication and Hospitality**

Establish clear communication channels with guests before, during, and after their stay to address any questions, concerns, or special requests promptly. Provide personalized recommendations for local attractions, restaurants, and activities to enhance the guest experience and foster positive reviews.

**Property Management**

Implement efficient property management practices to streamline operations and ensure a seamless guest experience. Consider outsourcing tasks such as cleaning, maintenance, key exchange, and guest communication to professional property management companies or service providers to save time and resources.

## Price Optimization

Continuously monitor market conditions, demand trends, and competitor pricing to optimize your rental rates and maximize occupancy and revenue. Adjust pricing dynamically based on factors such as seasonality, local events, holidays, and supply and demand dynamics to achieve optimal results.

## Guest Reviews and Feedback

Encourage guests to leave reviews and feedback after their stay to help improve your property's reputation and attract future guests. Respond to reviews promptly and professionally, addressing any concerns or issues raised by guests and demonstrating your commitment to providing exceptional hospitality.

## Compliance and Regulations

Familiarize yourself with local regulations, zoning laws, and homeowner association rules governing short-term rentals in your area. Ensure compliance with applicable laws and regulations, obtain any necessary permits or licenses, and adhere to safety and health standards to protect your guests and mitigate legal risks.

## Performance Evaluation and Optimization

Regularly evaluate the performance of your short-term rental properties by analyzing key performance indicators such as occupancy rates, average nightly rates, revenue, and guest satisfaction scores. Identify areas for improvement and implement strategies to optimize performance and maximize profitability over time.

By harnessing the power of short-term rentals and implementing effective strategies for property selection, marketing, guest communication, and operations management, investors can capitalize on the growing demand for short-term accommodation and generate significant returns on their real estate investments.

# Maximizing Returns with Commercial Properties

Maximizing returns with commercial properties is a sophisticated endeavor that requires a strategic approach, thorough market analysis, and astute management practices. Unlike residential properties, commercial real estate encompasses a diverse range of property types, including office buildings, retail spaces, industrial warehouses, and multifamily complexes, each with its unique set of opportunities and challenges.

One key aspect of maximizing returns with commercial properties is selecting the right investment opportunities. Investors must conduct comprehensive market research to identify markets and submarkets with strong economic fundamentals, demographic trends, and growth potential. Factors such as population growth, job creation, infrastructure development, and business expansion can impact the demand for commercial space and influence rental rates and property values.

Furthermore, investors must carefully evaluate the financial performance and potential of commercial properties before making investment decisions. This involves analyzing key performance indicators such as net operating income (NOI), cash flow, cap rates, and internal rates of return (IRR) to assess the property's income-generating potential and overall investment viability. Additionally, investors should consider factors such as lease terms, tenant quality, occupancy rates, and market comparables to gauge the property's value and growth prospects accurately.

Once an investment opportunity has been identified and acquired, maximizing returns with commercial properties requires effective asset management and optimization strategies. Investors must actively manage their properties to enhance value, minimize expenses, and maximize cash flow. This may involve implementing cost-saving initiatives, negotiating favorable lease terms, implementing value-add strategies such as property renovations or repositioning, and actively leasing vacant space to high-quality tenants.

Moreover, investors can leverage financing strategies such as debt refinancing, capital improvements, or property redevelopment to enhance property value and generate higher returns. By strategically deploying capital and optimizing property performance, investors can unlock hidden value within their commercial properties and achieve superior investment outcomes.

In addition to traditional property management strategies, investors can also explore innovative approaches to maximizing returns with commercial properties, such as incorporating technology solutions for operational efficiency, sustainability initiatives to reduce operating costs, and creative leasing structures to attract and retain tenants. Embracing emerging trends and market dynamics can position investors to capitalize on opportunities and stay ahead of the curve in the competitive commercial real estate landscape.

In summary, maximizing returns with commercial properties requires a holistic approach that encompasses thorough market analysis, strategic investment decisions, effective asset management, and innovative optimization strategies. By leveraging market insights, financial expertise, and operational excellence, investors can unlock the full potential of their commercial real estate investments and achieve superior returns over the long term.

# Uncovering Opportunities in Emerging Markets

Uncovering opportunities in emerging markets is an exciting endeavor that requires a blend of foresight, market intelligence, and strategic decision-making. Emerging markets, characterized by rapid economic growth, demographic shifts, and increasing urbanization, offer investors unique opportunities for growth and diversification. However, navigating these markets requires careful analysis and a deep understanding of local dynamics, risks, and potential rewards.

One key aspect of uncovering opportunities in emerging markets is conducting thorough market research to identify regions and sectors with high growth potential. This involves analyzing macroeconomic indicators such as GDP growth rates, inflation rates, employment trends, and consumer spending patterns to assess the overall health and trajectory of the market. Additionally, investors must evaluate market-specific factors such as political stability, regulatory environment, infrastructure development, and cultural nuances to gauge the investment landscape accurately.

Moreover, investors should pay close attention to demographic trends and urbanization patterns in emerging markets, as these factors can drive demand for various asset classes such as residential, commercial, and industrial properties. Rising incomes, expanding middle-class populations, and increasing urbanization rates often create demand for housing, retail, office, and logistics space, presenting opportunities for investment across the real estate spectrum.

Furthermore, investors can uncover opportunities in emerging markets by focusing on niche sectors or emerging trends that are poised for growth. This may involve targeting sectors such as technology, healthcare, renewable energy, e-commerce, or tourism, which are experiencing rapid expansion and disruption in emerging markets. By identifying underserved or overlooked market segments, investors can capitalize on untapped opportunities and gain a competitive advantage in the market.

In addition to traditional investment approaches, investors can also explore alternative investment vehicles such as private equity, venture capital, real estate funds, or infrastructure projects to gain exposure to emerging markets. These investment vehicles offer diversification benefits, access to specialized expertise, and potential for attractive risk-adjusted returns in high-growth sectors and regions.

However, uncovering opportunities in emerging markets also comes with risks and challenges that investors must carefully navigate. These may include currency fluctuations, political instability, regulatory hurdles, lack of transparency, and operational complexities. Therefore, it's essential for investors to conduct thorough due diligence, build local networks and partnerships, and implement risk management strategies to mitigate potential risks and enhance investment resilience.

In summary, uncovering opportunities in emerging markets requires a combination of market savvy, risk management, and strategic insight. By conducting thorough research, identifying growth drivers, and leveraging specialized expertise, investors can uncover hidden gems and capitalize on the growth potential of emerging markets while managing associated risks effectively. With the right approach and execution, investing in emerging markets can provide attractive returns and diversification benefits for investors seeking to expand their global investment portfolios.

# The Art of Negotiation in Real Estate Deals

The art of negotiation in real estate deals is a critical skill that can make the difference between a successful transaction and a missed opportunity. Whether you're buying, selling, leasing, or financing a property, effective negotiation can help you achieve your objectives, maximize value, and build mutually beneficial relationships with counterparties. Here's a detailed look at the key principles and strategies of negotiation in real estate deals:

**Preparation and Research**

Preparation is key to successful negotiation in real estate deals. Start by researching the market, property, and counterparties to understand their needs, motivations, and constraints. Gather information on recent comparable sales or leases, property condition, zoning regulations, financing options, and market trends to support your negotiation position.

**Set Clear Objectives**

Define your objectives and priorities for the negotiation, including price, terms, timelines, and contingencies. Identify your desired outcome and alternative options to leverage during the negotiation process. Establish clear boundaries and walk-away points to guide your decision-making and maintain negotiating leverage.

**Build Rapport and Trust**

Establishing rapport and trust with counterparties is essential for fostering open communication and building productive relationships. Listen actively, empathize with their concerns, and seek common ground to create a collaborative negotiating environment. Building rapport can help overcome obstacles, resolve conflicts, and reach mutually acceptable agreements.

**Focus on Value Creation**

Approach negotiation as a value-creating process rather than a zero-sum game. Look for opportunities to create value and trade-offs that benefit both parties. Explore creative solutions, incentives, and concessions that address the interests and priorities of all parties involved. By focusing on value creation, you can expand the pie and increase the likelihood of reaching a favorable outcome for all stakeholders.

**Effective Communication**

Communicate your needs, interests, and expectations clearly and persuasively during negotiations. Use active listening, empathy, and assertiveness to convey your message and understand the perspectives of counterparties. Choose your words carefully, maintain a positive tone, and avoid confrontational or adversarial language that can escalate tensions and hinder progress.

## Negotiate Win-Win Solutions

Strive to negotiate win-win solutions that satisfy the interests of both parties and preserve the relationship for future dealings. Seek to understand the underlying interests and motivations driving counterparties' positions and look for creative solutions that address their needs while advancing your own objectives. Collaborate on problem-solving and explore trade-offs that optimize outcomes for all parties involved.

## Flexibility and Adaptability

Remain flexible and adaptable throughout the negotiation process to respond to changing circumstances and new information. Be willing to adjust your strategy, priorities, and concessions as needed to overcome obstacles and reach a mutually acceptable agreement. Maintain a positive attitude and focus on finding common ground to keep negotiations moving forward.

## Negotiate with Authority and Confidence

Project confidence, professionalism, and authority during negotiations to convey your credibility and seriousness as a negotiator. Back up your positions with facts, data, and market knowledge to support your arguments and reinforce your negotiating leverage. Demonstrate your commitment to achieving a fair and equitable outcome while advocating for your interests assertively.

## Document and Formalize Agreements

Once an agreement has been reached, document the terms and conditions in writing and formalize the agreement through a legally binding contract. Ensure that all parties understand their rights, obligations, and responsibilities under the agreement and address any contingencies or potential issues upfront. Seek legal advice if necessary to review and finalize the contract to protect your interests.

By applying these principles and strategies of negotiation in real estate deals, you can enhance your effectiveness as a negotiator, achieve favorable outcomes, and build lasting relationships with counterparties. Whether you're negotiating a purchase price, lease terms, financing terms, or other aspects of a real estate transaction, mastering the art of negotiation can be a valuable asset in your real estate investment journey.

# Mitigating Risks and Protecting Your Investments

Mitigating risks and protecting your investments are essential aspects of successful real estate investing. While real estate can offer lucrative opportunities for wealth creation, it also comes with inherent risks that can impact investment returns and financial stability. Here's a comprehensive guide on how to mitigate risks and protect your investments in real estate:

**Diversification**

Diversifying your real estate portfolio across different property types, locations, and investment strategies can help spread risk and minimize exposure to market fluctuations. By diversifying your investments, you can reduce the impact of adverse events on your overall portfolio and increase resilience to market volatility.

## Thorough Due Diligence

Conducting thorough due diligence on potential investment opportunities is essential for identifying risks and evaluating investment viability. This involves analyzing factors such as property condition, location, market dynamics, financial performance, tenant quality, and regulatory compliance. Engage qualified professionals such as inspectors, appraisers, attorneys, and financial advisors to assist with due diligence efforts and ensure a comprehensive assessment of investment risks.

## Risk Assessment and Management

Identify and assess potential risks associated with each investment opportunity, including market risks, financial risks, operational risks, legal risks, and environmental risks. Develop risk mitigation strategies and contingency plans to address identified risks and minimize their impact on investment performance. Regularly monitor and review risks to proactively manage and mitigate potential threats to your investments.

**Conservative Financing**

Adopting conservative financing practices can help reduce leverage and minimize financial risk exposure in real estate investments. Avoid over-leveraging properties and maintain adequate reserves for unexpected expenses, vacancies, and economic downturns. Evaluate financing options carefully, consider fixed-rate loans with favorable terms, and avoid risky financial instruments that could expose you to interest rate fluctuations or payment shocks.

**Insurance Protection**

Investing in insurance coverage can provide an additional layer of protection against unforeseen events and liabilities. Consider obtaining property insurance, liability insurance, landlord insurance, and other relevant insurance policies to safeguard your investments against property damage, natural disasters, accidents, and legal claims. Review insurance policies regularly to ensure adequate coverage and compliance with insurance requirements.

**Legal Compliance**

Ensure compliance with applicable laws, regulations, and zoning ordinances governing real estate investments in your target markets. Familiarize yourself with landlord-tenant laws, fair housing regulations, building codes, environmental regulations, and other legal requirements to avoid potential penalties, fines, or litigation. Seek legal advice when drafting contracts, lease agreements, and other legal documents to protect your interests and mitigate legal risks.

**Property Maintenance and Risk Mitigation**

Implement proactive property maintenance practices to minimize the risk of property damage, safety hazards, and liability issues. Regularly inspect properties, address maintenance issues promptly, and invest in preventive maintenance measures to preserve property value and mitigate risks. Implement safety protocols, security measures, and emergency preparedness plans to protect tenants, employees, and visitors from potential risks and hazards.

**Professional Property Management**

Hiring professional property management services can help streamline operations, mitigate risks, and enhance the value of your real estate investments. Property managers can oversee day-to-day property operations, tenant relations, rent collection, maintenance, and repairs, freeing up your time and resources to focus on strategic decision-making and investment growth.

## Continuous Monitoring and Adaptation

Stay vigilant and proactive in monitoring market conditions, economic trends, and investment performance to identify emerging risks and opportunities. Stay informed about industry developments, regulatory changes, and market dynamics that could impact your investments. Be prepared to adapt your investment strategy, asset allocation, and risk management approach accordingly to navigate changing market conditions effectively.

## Exit Strategies and Contingency Planning

Develop exit strategies and contingency plans to mitigate potential risks and uncertainties associated with real estate investments. Consider alternative scenarios, such as property appreciation, market downturns, tenant defaults, or unexpected events, and prepare contingency plans to mitigate potential losses or capitalize on opportunities. Evaluate options for refinancing, selling, or repurposing properties to optimize returns and minimize risks in different market conditions.

By implementing these risk mitigation strategies and protective measures, you can safeguard your real estate investments, preserve capital, and enhance long-term investment success. While it's impossible to eliminate all risks entirely, proactive risk management and prudent decision-making can help mitigate potential threats and position you for sustainable growth and profitability in your real estate portfolio.

# Scaling Your Portfolio for Long-Term Success

Scaling your real estate portfolio for long-term success involves strategic planning, disciplined execution, and prudent risk management. As you seek to expand your portfolio, it's essential to consider factors such as market dynamics, investment objectives, financing options, and risk tolerance. Here's a detailed guide on how to scale your real estate portfolio for long-term success:

**Define Your Investment Strategy**

Clarify your investment goals, objectives, and criteria for portfolio expansion. Determine your target markets, property types, investment strategies, and desired risk-return profile. Consider factors such as cash flow, appreciation potential, leverage, diversification, and exit strategies to align your investment strategy with your long-term financial goals.

## Market Research and Analysis

Conduct comprehensive market research to identify opportunities and trends in your target markets. Analyze market fundamentals such as supply and demand dynamics, population growth, job creation, rental yields, and economic indicators to assess market viability and investment potential. Stay informed about local market conditions, emerging trends, and regulatory changes that could impact investment decisions.

## Portfolio Diversification

Diversify your real estate portfolio across different property types, locations, and investment strategies to spread risk and enhance resilience. Consider investing in residential, commercial, industrial, and mixed-use properties across diverse geographic regions to mitigate exposure to local market risks and economic cycles. Explore alternative asset classes such as real estate investment trusts (REITs), crowdfunding platforms, or private equity funds to further diversify your portfolio and access new opportunities.

**Strategic Acquisitions and Dispositions**

Identify strategic acquisition opportunities that align with your investment strategy and growth objectives. Look for properties with value-add potential, below-market rents, distressed conditions, or redevelopment opportunities that can generate attractive returns. Similarly, consider divesting underperforming or non-strategic assets to free up capital, streamline your portfolio, and reinvest in higher-yielding opportunities. Evaluate potential acquisitions and dispositions based on financial analysis, market research, and due diligence to optimize portfolio performance and achieve long-term growth objectives.

**Financing Strategies**

Explore financing options such as mortgages, loans, lines of credit, or partnerships to fund portfolio expansion. Evaluate financing terms, interest rates, loan-to-value ratios, and repayment schedules to optimize leverage and mitigate financial risks. Consider alternative financing sources such as private lenders, hard money lenders, or crowdfunding platforms to access capital and facilitate property acquisitions. Maintain a prudent debt-to-equity ratio and reserve funds for debt service coverage, capital expenditures, and contingencies to safeguard financial stability and liquidity.

**Operational Efficiency and Scalability**

Implement scalable operational systems, processes, and technologies to streamline portfolio management and optimize efficiency. Utilize property management software, accounting systems, and customer relationship management (CRM) tools to automate routine tasks, track performance metrics, and improve decision-making. Standardize operating procedures, tenant communications, and maintenance protocols to enhance productivity and scalability as your portfolio grows. Leverage economies of scale, centralized services, and outsourcing opportunities to reduce costs, increase profitability, and maximize returns on investment.

**Risk Management and Contingency Planning**

Implement robust risk management strategies to identify, assess, and mitigate potential risks associated with portfolio expansion. Conduct thorough due diligence on prospective investments, tenants, and counterparties to evaluate creditworthiness, legal compliance, and operational risks. Maintain adequate insurance coverage, reserves, and contingency plans for unforeseen events such as property damage, tenant defaults, or economic downturns. Monitor market conditions, economic indicators, and industry trends to proactively manage risks and adjust investment strategies accordingly.

## Continuous Learning and Adaptation

Stay informed about industry developments, market trends, and emerging opportunities to adapt and evolve your investment strategy over time. Invest in ongoing education, professional development, and networking opportunities to expand your knowledge, skills, and network within the real estate industry. Learn from past experiences, successes, and failures to refine your approach, optimize performance, and achieve long-term success in scaling your real estate portfolio.

By following these strategies and principles, you can scale your real estate portfolio for long-term success and achieve your financial goals. With careful planning, disciplined execution, and prudent risk management, you can build a diversified and resilient portfolio that generates sustainable income, preserves capital, and creates wealth over time.

# Embracing Technology for Property Management

Embracing technology for property management has become increasingly essential in the modern real estate landscape, revolutionizing the way properties are managed, maintained, and marketed. By leveraging innovative technologies and software solutions, property managers can streamline operations, enhance tenant experiences, and optimize portfolio performance. Here's a comprehensive exploration of how technology is transforming property management:

Innovative property management software platforms offer a centralized hub for managing various aspects of property operations, including leasing, rent collection, maintenance, accounting, and communication. These platforms enable property managers to automate routine tasks, track critical metrics, and streamline workflows, saving time and increasing operational efficiency. By digitizing processes such as lease administration, tenant onboarding, and work order management, property managers can reduce administrative overhead, minimize errors, and improve productivity.

One of the most significant benefits of embracing technology for property management is the ability to enhance tenant experiences and satisfaction. Tenant portals and mobile apps provide tenants with convenient access to essential services, such as online rent payments, maintenance requests, lease documents, and community announcements. By offering self-service options and 24/7 support channels, property managers can improve tenant engagement, communication, and retention rates. Additionally, automated communication tools enable property managers to send timely reminders, updates, and notifications to tenants, fostering transparency and trust.

Moreover, technology-driven solutions enable property managers to proactively monitor and maintain properties, reducing downtime, minimizing disruptions, and preserving asset value. Internet of Things (IoT) devices, such as smart thermostats, sensors, and meters, allow property managers to remotely monitor energy usage, detect leaks, and optimize building performance in real time. Predictive maintenance software analyzes equipment data and performance metrics to identify potential issues before they escalate, enabling proactive repairs and minimizing costly downtime.

Furthermore, technology plays a crucial role in marketing and leasing properties, enabling property managers to reach a broader audience, attract qualified tenants, and optimize occupancy rates. Digital marketing channels, such as property listing websites, social media platforms, and online advertising, allow property managers to showcase properties effectively and target prospective tenants with tailored messaging. Virtual tours, 3D renderings, and video walkthroughs provide immersive experiences that engage prospective tenants and differentiate properties in competitive markets.

Data analytics and business intelligence tools empower property managers to make informed decisions, optimize portfolio performance, and identify opportunities for growth. By collecting and analyzing data on tenant preferences, market trends, rental rates, and financial metrics, property managers can gain valuable insights into property performance and market dynamics. These insights enable property managers to optimize pricing strategies, identify cost-saving opportunities, and allocate resources effectively to maximize returns on investment.

In conclusion, embracing technology for property management offers numerous benefits for property managers, landlords, and tenants alike. By adopting innovative software solutions, leveraging data-driven insights, and embracing digital marketing channels, property managers can streamline operations, enhance tenant experiences, and optimize portfolio performance. As technology continues to evolve, property managers must remain agile and adaptable, embracing new tools and strategies to stay competitive in an increasingly digital world.

# Creating Passive Income Streams with Real Estate Syndication

Creating passive income streams with real estate syndication offers investors an opportunity to participate in lucrative real estate investments without the challenges of direct property ownership or management. Real estate syndication involves pooling funds from multiple investors to acquire, manage, and profit from income-producing properties. This collaborative approach allows individual investors to access larger, more diversified, and potentially higher-yielding real estate assets than they could on their own. Here's a comprehensive exploration of how real estate syndication creates passive income streams for investors:

Firstly, real estate syndication typically involves the formation of a legal entity, such as a limited liability company (LLC) or limited partnership (LP), to facilitate the investment. A general partner or sponsor, typically an experienced real estate professional or firm, identifies and structures investment opportunities, conducts due diligence, and manages the day-to-day operations of the investment. Limited partners, or passive investors, contribute capital to the syndication and receive ownership interests or shares in return.

One of the primary benefits of real estate syndication is the ability to generate passive income through rental income distributions and potential appreciation of the underlying properties. Syndicated real estate investments often target income-producing assets such as multifamily apartment buildings, office buildings, retail centers, or industrial warehouses, which generate steady cash flow from rental income. Passive investors receive regular distributions of rental income proportionate to their ownership stake in the syndication, providing a reliable source of passive income.

Moreover, real estate syndication allows investors to leverage the expertise, resources, and economies of scale of the sponsor or general partner. Experienced sponsors bring market knowledge, deal sourcing capabilities, and operational expertise to the table, enhancing the likelihood of success and minimizing risks for passive investors. Sponsors handle property acquisition, financing, asset management, leasing, and disposition, allowing passive investors to benefit from professional management without the burden of day-to-day responsibilities.

Furthermore, real estate syndication offers investors access to a diversified portfolio of real estate assets across different property types, geographic markets, and investment strategies. By participating in syndicated investments, investors can spread risk and reduce exposure to individual property or market risks. Diversification helps protect investors against unforeseen events, market downturns, or property-specific challenges, enhancing the resilience and stability of their investment portfolios.

Additionally, real estate syndication provides passive investors with opportunities for potential tax benefits and wealth accumulation. Syndicated real estate investments may offer tax advantages such as depreciation deductions, pass-through losses, and capital gains deferral opportunities, which can help optimize tax efficiency and maximize after-tax returns for investors. Moreover, real estate syndication allows investors to build equity and wealth over time through property appreciation, mortgage paydown, and value-added strategies implemented by the sponsor.

In conclusion, real estate syndication offers investors a powerful vehicle for creating passive income streams and building wealth through real estate investments. By pooling resources, leveraging professional expertise, and accessing diversified portfolios of income-producing properties, investors can generate steady cash flow, mitigate risks, and achieve long-term financial goals. As with any investment, it's essential for investors to conduct thorough due diligence, evaluate the track record and credibility of sponsors, and align investment opportunities with their risk tolerance and investment objectives. With careful consideration and prudent decision-making, real estate syndication can be a valuable addition to an investor's passive income strategy.

# Tax Strategies for Real Estate Investors

Tax strategies play a crucial role in optimizing returns and maximizing profitability for real estate investors. By leveraging tax advantages and implementing strategic planning, investors can minimize tax liabilities, enhance cash flow, and improve overall investment performance. Here's a comprehensive exploration of tax strategies for real estate investors:

Firstly, one of the most significant tax advantages of real estate investing is depreciation. Depreciation allows investors to deduct the cost of acquiring income-producing properties over time, reducing taxable income and lowering tax liabilities. Investors can depreciate the value of residential rental properties over 27.5 years and commercial properties over 39 years, providing a valuable tax deduction that offsets rental income and improves cash flow.

Moreover, real estate investors can take advantage of tax-deferred exchanges, such as 1031 exchanges, to defer capital gains taxes on the sale of investment properties. By reinvesting proceeds from the sale into like-kind replacement properties within specified timeframes, investors can defer capital gains taxes indefinitely, allowing them to reinvest gains and grow their real estate portfolios without immediate tax consequences.

Additionally, real estate investors can utilize cost segregation studies to accelerate depreciation deductions and optimize tax savings. Cost segregation involves identifying and reclassifying certain components of a property, such as fixtures, finishes, and equipment, to shorter depreciation schedules. By accelerating depreciation deductions, investors can reduce taxable income and generate significant tax savings in the early years of property ownership.

Furthermore, real estate investors may qualify for various tax credits and incentives designed to promote investment in certain types of properties or geographic areas. For example, investors in low-income housing projects may be eligible for the Low-Income Housing Tax Credit (LIHTC), which provides a dollar-for-dollar reduction in federal income tax liability for each dollar of eligible project costs incurred. Similarly, investors in historic rehabilitation projects may qualify for the Federal Historic Rehabilitation Tax Credit, which provides a tax credit equal to a percentage of eligible rehabilitation expenses.

In addition to federal tax benefits, real estate investors should also consider state-specific tax incentives and deductions that may be available. Many states offer property tax exemptions, credits, or abatements for certain types of properties, such as affordable housing, historic properties, or renewable energy projects. By taking advantage of state tax incentives, investors can further enhance tax savings and improve investment returns.

Furthermore, real estate investors should engage with tax professionals, such as certified public accountants (CPAs) or tax advisors, to develop and implement tax-efficient investment strategies. Tax professionals can provide personalized guidance, advice, and tax planning services tailored to investors' specific circumstances and objectives. They can help investors navigate complex tax laws, maximize available deductions and credits, and ensure compliance with regulatory requirements.

In conclusion, tax strategies are essential for optimizing returns and maximizing profitability for real estate investors. By leveraging tax advantages such as depreciation, 1031 exchanges, cost segregation, and tax credits, investors can minimize tax liabilities, enhance cash flow, and improve overall investment performance. Working with experienced tax professionals and staying informed about relevant tax laws and incentives can help investors develop effective tax strategies that align with their investment goals and objectives.

# The Future of Passive Income in Real Estate

The future of passive income in real estate is poised for significant transformation, driven by technological advancements, changing consumer preferences, and evolving market dynamics. As we look ahead, several trends are likely to shape the landscape of passive income generation in real estate:

Firstly, technology will continue to play a pivotal role in revolutionizing how real estate is managed, marketed, and monetized. Innovations such as artificial intelligence, big data analytics, blockchain technology, and the Internet of Things (IoT) are empowering property owners and investors to streamline operations, enhance tenant experiences, and optimize portfolio performance. From smart buildings and predictive maintenance to digital marketing and online property management platforms, technology-driven solutions will enable investors to generate passive income more efficiently and effectively than ever before.

Moreover, the rise of alternative investment platforms, such as real estate crowdfunding and peer-to-peer lending, is democratizing access to real estate investments and expanding opportunities for passive income generation. These platforms allow individual investors to pool their resources and participate in a diverse range of real estate projects, from residential and commercial properties to development projects and income-producing assets. By leveraging the power of technology and collective investment, investors can access previously inaccessible markets, diversify their portfolios, and generate passive income with relatively low barriers to entry.

Additionally, the shift towards remote work and digital nomadism is reshaping demand patterns and investment opportunities in the real estate market.

As more people embrace flexible work arrangements and prioritize lifestyle choices, there is growing demand for residential properties in suburban and rural areas, as well as vacation rentals and short-term accommodation in desirable destinations. Investors can capitalize on these trends by targeting properties that cater to remote workers, digital nomads, and lifestyle-oriented tenants, generating passive income from rental yields and appreciation potential.

Furthermore, sustainable and eco-friendly real estate investments are gaining traction as investors prioritize environmental, social, and governance (ESG) considerations in their investment decisions. Green buildings, energy-efficient technologies, and sustainable development projects offer opportunities for passive income generation while promoting environmental stewardship and social responsibility. Investors can capitalize on the growing demand for sustainable real estate assets by incorporating ESG criteria into their investment strategies and targeting properties with strong sustainability credentials.

Moreover, regulatory and policy changes, such as tax incentives for renewable energy projects, affordable housing initiatives, and urban revitalization programs, will continue to influence investment opportunities and passive income strategies in real estate. Investors should stay informed about legislative developments, regulatory changes, and government incentives that may impact real estate investments and adjust their strategies accordingly to optimize returns and mitigate risks.

In conclusion, the future of passive income in real estate is characterized by technological innovation, market diversification, and sustainability-driven investment strategies. By embracing emerging trends, leveraging technology, and staying attuned to evolving market dynamics, investors can position themselves to capitalize on new opportunities and generate sustainable passive income streams in the dynamic and ever-changing real estate landscape.

# Conclusion

In conclusion, "Passive Income Pulse: Real Estate Tactics for Thriving in Today's Market" serves as a comprehensive guide for investors seeking to harness the power of real estate to generate passive income and build long-term wealth. Throughout this book, we have explored a diverse range of strategies, techniques, and insights designed to help investors navigate today's dynamic real estate landscape and achieve their financial goals.

From understanding the fundamentals of passive income paradigms to embracing cutting-edge technology for property management, each chapter has provided valuable insights and practical advice to empower investors to succeed in their real estate endeavors. Whether you're a seasoned investor looking to scale your portfolio or a novice seeking to embark on your real estate journey, this book has equipped you with the knowledge, tools, and strategies needed to thrive in today's competitive market.

As we look to the future, the opportunities for passive income generation in real estate are abundant and ever-evolving. By staying informed, adaptable, and strategic, investors can leverage emerging trends, technological innovations, and market dynamics to capitalize on new opportunities and unlock the full potential of their real estate investments.

I hope that the insights shared in this book will inspire you to take action, think creatively, and embark on your journey towards financial freedom through real estate investing. Whether you're building a diversified portfolio of income-producing properties, exploring innovative investment vehicles such as real estate syndication, or leveraging tax strategies to optimize returns, the principles and tactics outlined in this book will serve as a roadmap for success in your pursuit of passive income in real estate.

Thank you for joining me on this journey, and may your ventures in real estate investing be prosperous and fulfilling.

www.ingramcontent.com/pod-product-compliance
Lightning Source LLC
Chambersburg PA
CBHW071950210526
45479CB00003B/874